KAMMIE ON FIRST

KAMMIE ON FIRST

Baseball's Dottie Kamenshek

Michelle Houts

BIOGRAPHIES FOR YOUNG READERS

OHIO UNIVERSITY PRESS

Athens

Ohio University Press, Athens, Ohio 45701
ohioswallow.com

Printed in the United States of America
Ohio University Press books are printed on acid-free paper ∞ ™

24 23 22 21 20 19 18 17 16 15 14   5 4 3 2 1

Frontispiece: Kammie smiles for the camera. *Photo courtesy of Center for History, South Bend, IN*

Library of Congress Cataloging-in-Publication Data

Houts, Michelle.
 Kammie on first : baseball's Dottie Kamenshek / Michelle Houts.
     pages cm.—(Biographies for young readers)
 Includes bibliographical references and index.
 ISBN 978-0-8214-2133-8 (hardback)—ISBN 978-0-8214-2130-7 (pb)—
ISBN 978-0-8214-4511-2 (pdf)
 1. Kamenshek, Dorothy, 1925–2010. 2. Baseball players—United States—Biography.
3. Women baseball players—United States—Biography. 4. All-American Girls Profes-
sional Baseball League—History. I. Title.
 GV865.K317H68 2014
 796.357092—dc23
 [B]
                                2014029645

CONTENTS

AUTHOR'S NOTES

I HAVE A vivid memory of a summer night. It could have been any of dozens of summer nights in the early 1970s. In fact, it's quite likely that it is a composite memory of several such nights.

It's a humid, sticky Ohio sundown. I'm about six years old. My sisters and I have had our baths and we're wearing cotton nightgowns. In the house, all the windows are open, but no air moves. It's time for bed, but even our mother agrees it's just too hot in our upstairs bedrooms to sleep.

In the family room, a fan stirs the warmth around, making a hot breeze that feels better than no breeze at all. We're allowed to stay up, if we're quiet. On one end of the couch sits my father, a pad of graph paper on his lap, pipe in one hand, pencil in the other. And on the end table beside him is the radio.

We're allowed to stay up. If we're quiet. Because the Cincinnati Reds are playing. My younger sister and I can both fit on the other end of the couch without disturbing our father, who leans closer to the radio. The only television we own is in the room, but the game is not on TV. So the TV stays off.

Over the radio, Al Michaels tells us what's happening. *There's the pitch.* Silence. *Outside.* Silence. *A low fastball from the mound.* Silence. *Strike.* His voice is familiar. We've heard it often. It's the voice of hot summer nights in Ohio. And though I know almost nothing about what he's saying, I like the way it sounds. The names: Bench, Concepción, Perez, Gerónimo, Rose. The words: triple play, sacrifice, full count. I don't know what they mean, but my dad will explain. Later. When he's not listening. When he's not making marks on his graph paper.

Outside the crickets sing. A June bug hits the screen door. And the fan sends the night's first cool breeze across my forehead, lifting my bangs just a little. And Al Michaels tells us what's happening. *A line drive to left field.* Silence. *There's the throw to second.* Silence. *He's safe.* Al Michaels tells us what's happening. My eyes grow heavy. I can still listen with them closed. *Here's the pitch.* Silence.

Some kids become baseball fans on the diamond, in the outfield, or playing backyard pitch-and-catch, but I became a baseball fan falling asleep by the radio. I'll admit that to call myself a baseball fan might not be completely accurate, as my interest in any sport has always been somewhat singular. I only cared about baseball if the Cincinnati Reds were playing. Football and basketball? Not interested unless it's the Ohio State Buckeyes. I never played sports myself, preferring to read or write stories instead.

So, when I learned about a Cincinnati girl who loved the Reds and went on to become one of the very best women in baseball, I was intrigued. Kammie's life seemed, at first, too obscure to fill a biography. She was quiet. Her talent made the fans in the stands go wild, but she was always calm. She was humble, so she didn't seek out attention. Only a few interviews exist. Her family was small. Her memorabilia, inaccessible.

But it didn't take long to learn that Kammie did leave us a legacy. She left people who cared deeply for her, people who looked up to her for the incredible player and big-hearted human being she was. She helped others. She taught others. She shared her life with others. And they, in turn, shared with me the reasons they admired her. In the end, what Kammie left behind for the rest of us was more than simply enough to fill a biography.

ACKNOWLEDGMENTS

THIS BIOGRAPHY was a team effort. Key players included Kammie's contemporaries: All-Americans Betsy Jochum, Helen Waddell Wyatt, and Katie Horstman who met with me, sharing their memories and memorabilia. Many former Peaches granted telephone interviews, graciously giving me their play-by-play accounts of life in the All-American Girls Professional Baseball League. I had great coaches in authors Sue Macy, Merrie Fidler, and Susan E. Johnson, whose books were the foundation of my understanding of the AAGPBL. The team was well managed by the folks at Ohio University Press, who had a vision and trusted me with the first at-bat. And then, of course, there are the fans. My husband, Mark, and children, Olivia, Seth, and Maggie, and travel companion Jodi, who kept cheering me on even when I was sure I had struck out.

Thank you, readers, for your curiosity, for wanting to know more about this Cincinnati girl who made good. You've got the best seat in the house. I hope you enjoy the game.

REGULATION
GAME

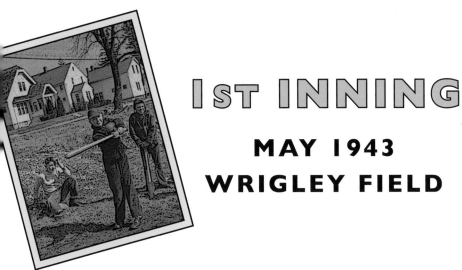

1st INNING

MAY 1943
WRIGLEY FIELD

"I thought, 'This is my chance.'[1] I just gave it my best and kept my mouth shut."[2]

—Dottie Kamenshek

BALLS WHIZZED in all directions. Wrigley Field, one of America's best-known Major League ballparks, was abuzz with activity. Outfielders darted left and right to recover balls purposely hit to make them scramble. Pitchers showed off their best moves while catchers dove to the dirt. It might have seemed like a typical day of tryouts for Philip K. Wrigley's Chicago Cubs, except that the only men at the park that day were **scouts,**★ coaches, and managers.

The 280 players on the field were women. "Girls," as they were commonly referred to in those days, who had traveled to Chicago, Illinois, from twenty-six states and even from Canada to take a shot at being selected for the brand new All-American Girls

★All words defined in the glossary will be set in bold type when they first appear within the book.

Softball League. Some came from cities, and some were farm girls. Some were married with husbands stationed overseas in World War II. Some were teenagers barely out of high school.

Each was there with one goal: to play professional ball.

Dorothy Kamenshek, whose friends called her Dottie, was just seventeen years old. An outfielder from Cincinnati, Ohio, Dottie knew she had been given the opportunity of a lifetime. She, like many of the other girls at Wrigley Field that day, had already been through one round of tryouts back in her hometown. In Cincinnati, the players were asked what two positions they could play.

"I'd always been an outfielder," recalled Dottie. She wasn't sure what to tell the scouts. "Well, I thought, what does a left-hander do if she doesn't pitch except play outfield and first base? So, I told 'em first base."[3]

Dottie's performance at first base and in the outfield in Cincinnati had been enough to earn the trip to Chicago. She boarded a train with five other Cincinnati girls. To Dottie, Chicago was another world. Cincinnati was not a small town, but Chicago was enormous. Back at home, Dottie had never eaten out in a restaurant. Chicago was filled with new and exciting experiences!

Unfortunately, one of Dottie's first experiences at tryouts was not a good one. Her ball glove was stolen on one of the first days, and she had to borrow another from someone to finish tryouts. After that, things got better. She played some of the best ball she'd ever played. She wanted to be sure that if she wasn't chosen, it wouldn't be for lack of trying her best.

The beautiful Belmont Hotel, located just a few blocks from the ballpark, was the girls' home away from home for the week of tryouts. Dottie and the others walked to and from the hotel wearing skirts and sweaters, then changed in the locker rooms into pants and sweatshirts.

For a week, the girls vied for spots on four original teams. They participated in all sorts of drills designed to separate the good players from the great players.

"You played your position, you ran, you slid, you did everything," Dottie recalled.[4]

She also remembered the heartbreak that occurred each time a player was let go. Players with less potential were being cut from the very start. In her hotel room in the evenings, Dottie was afraid to answer the phone for fear she'd be told she'd been eliminated.

On a rainy Chicago morning at the end of the week, the remaining girls gathered around a chalkboard in the hotel lobby. They called it "allocation day." The luckiest girls would be assigned a new hometown. *Racine, Rockford, South Bend, Kenosha,* the headings read, with players' names listed below. Dottie stood in the crowd, eager to find her own name on one of the lists, knowing that if she didn't, she would be going home.

Finally, she saw it. *Rockford,* it said.

Dottie Kamenshek had become a Rockford Peach!

World War II, Chewing Gum, and Girls' Baseball

IN 1942, America was at war. All Americans were called upon to support the war effort at home and overseas. New cars were no longer manufactured so that steel could be saved to build ships and airplanes. Gasoline was **rationed**, meaning families had to limit their travels. Many youngsters in 1942 had already lived through the Great **Depression**. They were used to finding their own fun at home, in backyards, streets, and neighborhoods. And many children—boys and girls alike—played baseball.

Before the beginning of the 1942 Major League Baseball season, team owners and public officials alike began to fear for the future of men's baseball. Many able-bodied young ballplayers had enlisted to fight for the American cause. Would there be a shortage of players?

Another concern was on the minds of the Major League Baseball team owners and managers. How would it look if folks at home were playing games while their brothers and uncles were off fighting? The debate continued until a letter from the president of the United States gave everyone the green light to continue to enjoy America's favorite pastime.

President Franklin Roosevelt responded to a letter from Judge Kenesaw Mountain Landis, baseball's commissioner at the time.

"I honestly feel it would be best for the country to keep baseball going," the president wrote. *"There will be fewer people unemployed and everybody will work longer hours and harder than ever before. And that*

During the Depression it was common for children to play baseball in school-yards, vacant lots, and on city streets. *From the Harold Dobberpuhl Photo Collection. Photo courtesy of the Cedar-burg Cultural Center, Cedarburg, WI.*

means that they ought to have a chance for recreation and for taking their minds off their work even more than before."[5]

But even the president's blessing couldn't change the fact that many of baseball's best players would head off to war. Major League Baseball might continue, but who would play?

One team owner was particularly uncertain about the future of his ball club. Philip K. Wrigley owned two very popular enterprises: the Chicago Cubs and Wrigley's chewing gum. Philip Wrigley didn't mind that his players were leaving to fight for the American cause. In fact, he was an enthusiastic supporter of the war effort. Before any public rationing even took place, Mr. Wrigley voluntarily took down the enormous floodlights that illuminated the giant Wrigley Building in Chicago and gave them to the Navy to use. He donated to the military thousands of pounds of aluminum that would have been used to make chewing gum wrappers. And, he allowed the use of his company's prepaid radio time to advertise the war effort instead of Wrigley's spearmint gum.

It was Philip Wrigley's idea that if men's baseball in America were to come to a halt, perhaps the fans would enjoy watching professional women's softball. By the fall of 1942, he had a plan. He would create a girls' softball league like America had never seen. From the start, Mr. Wrigley knew just what he wanted and how his league would be different.

In the spring of 1943, Philip Wrigley sent his scouts to cities all over the Midwest and Canada. Their assignment? Find the best female softball players in America and Canada and give them a train ticket to Chicago. In all, the scouts managed to attract 280 hopeful young ladies from twenty-six states and five Canadian provinces. But only 64 would be allowed to stay. The rest were sent home with a story to tell about how they almost became a member of the All-American Girls Softball League.

As it turned out, Major League Baseball never did cease during the Second World War. It limped through the war years with fewer players, some much older or younger than the men they replaced. But while men's baseball was just surviving, the All-American Girls Professional Baseball League was exploding. The league was gaining fans by the thousands and making celebrities out of small-town girls who just loved to play ball.

Did you know? In 1940, Wrigley's chewing gum business made a profit of more than $8 million! It's no wonder Philip K. Wrigley had the funds to start a new baseball league.

2ND INNING

THE MAKING OF AN ALL-AMERICAN

"We just chose up sides and played!"[1]

—Dottie Kamenshek

L ET'S GO back a few years. Before World War II, before the Great Depression, before Philip K. Wrigley had even thought of starting a professional league for women.

It was 1925. Calvin Coolidge was president of the United States. American athletes had just brought home forty-five gold medals from the previous summer's Olympic Games in Paris, France. A new novel, *The Great Gatsby,* was published by popular author F. Scott Fitzgerald. And, in Norwood, Ohio, Dorothy Mary Kamenshek was born.

Dottie was the first and only child of immigrants who settled in the Cincinnati, Ohio, area. Her father, Nikolaus Kamenshek, came to the United States from Hungary when he was just twenty years old aboard the SS *George Washington,* an enormous ocean liner built to carry 2,900 passengers.

Passengers aboard the SS *George Washington* celebrate departure from the Port of New York by throwing ticker tape. *Photo courtesy of Library of Congress LC-B2- 2193-15.*

Dottie's mother, Johanna Bandenburg, was born in Ciacova, Romania. In 1918, Romania and Hungary were at war over land that bordered the two countries. When the fighting ended in 1920, many Romanians and Hungarians were tired of war and the devastation it left behind. Johanna's older sister, Catherine, had already left Romania with hopes of a better life in United States. Catherine had settled in Cincinnati and married a man named Charles Cook.

On a winter day in February, 1921, a ship called the SS *Calabria* arrived in the Port of New York. One of its passengers was 22-year-old Johanna Bandenburg. The ship's **manifest** indicated that Johanna was traveling alone and had paid for her own ticket. Her final destination was entered as the Cincinnati, Ohio, home of her brother-in-law, Mr. Charles Cook. And, in the place on the manifest in which passengers were asked about the length of their stay, Johanna's intentions were clearly marked: Forever.

The ships that carried Dottie's parents to the United States were typical ocean liners. They boasted beautiful first-class accommodations for some, and third-class and "steerage" accommodations for others. While first-class passengers slept in luxury cabins and took their meals on fine china in spacious dining rooms, steerage passengers endured cramped conditions well below deck. As the accommodations descended into the bowels of the ship, the price of the ticket also became cheaper. Both Nikolaus and Johanna were listed on their ships' registries as steerage passengers. If they were like many European emigrants of that era, they probably spent most of their savings on their tickets.

In Cincinnati, Johanna Bandenburg met Nikolaus Kamenshek. They were married on June 25, 1924. A year and a half later, on December 21, 1925, Dorothy was born. Her father worked as a barber while her mother took care of the home and young Dorothy. Nikolaus Kamenshek suffered from asthma for years. Sadly, when Dorothy was just nine years old, her father became more seriously ill. He died in 1935, leaving Dottie and her mother alone.

Dottie's family home on Marburg Avenue in Cincinnati, Ohio, where she lived in 1935 when her father passed away, is still standing today. *Photo by Michelle Houts.*

But the two were not lonely for long. Dottie's mother soon married another Hungarian gentleman, a tailor named Josef Wiener. It looked as if the family had a bright future ahead of them, but on August 30, 1937, Mr. Wiener became suddenly very ill. At Good Samaritan Hospital in Cincinnati, his appendix was removed in emergency surgery. But it was already too late. He died two days later, leaving Johanna a widow for the second time in two years and Dottie without a father once more.

Dottie's mother was a strong woman. Although she had attended school in Romania only until the third grade, she was

The Great Depression

WHEN Dottie was born, America appeared to be financially sound. But just before her fourth birthday, everything changed. The **stock market** crash of 1929 sent the United States into a great economic depression. Many factories and businesses laid off workers as consumers stopped purchasing their goods. In Cincinnati, Ohio, the Kamenshek family felt the effects of the depression like every other family. Dottie's father was a barber. Many small businesses suffered as people looked for ways to save pennies. If a man's wife or mother could cut his hair for free, why should he go to the barber and pay to have it cut?

Herbert Hoover was president when the Great Depression began. Many people lost their homes because, without jobs, they could no longer pay the **mortgage**. Homeless families found empty buildings, sheds, and tents to live in, most without electricity or plumbing. These small neighborhoods of displaced men, women, and children became known as "Hoovervilles." It would be many years before some families would be able to afford a home again.

Luckily, Dottie's family never lost their home. Still, Dottie recalled growing up "poor."[2] Her parents, eventually just her mother, had to work hard for everything the family had.

Betsy Jochum, another All-American Professional player, also grew up in Cincinnati during the depression. Just like Dottie, she remembers playing baseball with the boys in the streets and in empty lots. Sometimes just finding a ball and a bat was difficult, but someone would always show up with a single old ball or cracked bat and the game would begin. And when the cover fell off the ball, they would wrap it in tape and keep playing.

resourceful and independent. Despite being twice widowed, Johanna was determined to take care of herself and her young daughter. At the time, jobs were difficult for men to find, and it was even harder for a woman to find work outside her home. When Johanna was offered a job cleaning at a local soap factory—Procter and Gamble—she was grateful. She remained there for many years.

While Johanna worked, Dottie's days were filled with school and playing with the other children who lived nearby. She walked to school, and went home for lunch every day. In order to get home, eat lunch, and get back to school in the time allowed, Dottie had to run. She was a fast runner, even at ten years old.

Dottie's life as a child was different from other children her age. Dottie had an immigrant mother, who was still becoming accustomed to American culture and the English language. Many of Dottie's friends had mothers who were full-time homemakers. But Dottie's mother worked. And Johanna's work schedule meant Dottie was alone after school, something unheard of at the time. Dottie was learning how to be independent.

At ten years old, Dottie realized she was the only girl in her neighborhood. Rather than sit at home alone, she decided to join the boys at their game: **sandlot** baseball. The boys didn't seem to mind that she was the only girl on the team.

As a teenager at St. Bernard High, Dottie was quiet and serious. She was a member of the Girls' Athletic Association for four years. She played basketball because it was one of the only sports

Dottie was active in several clubs in high school, including basketball, typing, and track, and was a member of the yearbook staff. *Photo from the 1943* St. Bernardian.

available for girls. There was no girls' softball team. Since playing on the boys' baseball team wasn't an option, Dottie looked for other ways to play her favorite sport. That's when she learned about the industrial leagues in Cincinnati. Most factories and other large businesses sponsored a softball team, and Dottie was glad to get a chance to play for the H. H. Meyer Packing Company.

Dottie was a center fielder for the Meyer team, which had a successful run in the early 1940s. Dottie and her teammates made it to the finals in Detroit and Chicago three years in a row. One year, the H. H. Meyer girls lost to a team from Arizona in the finals. But another year, they beat a team from Richmond, Virginia, for the championship. These outings were a big deal to high school girls from Cincinnati who had little opportunity to travel.

Although it might not seem likely that a single mother from Romania would be much of a baseball fan, Dottie's mother was.

Perhaps it was a result of her daughter's love of the game, or maybe it was because the family lived in Cincinnati, a town that cherished their Major League Baseball team, the Cincinnati Reds. The Reds won the National League championship in 1940, when Dottie was a high school freshman, and they remained one of the top four teams in the league throughout Dottie's high school career. Johanna took her daughter to Ladies' Day at Crosley Field.

To Dottie, being in the stands on Ladies' Day wasn't simply a form of entertainment. It was an opportunity to observe the big-league players she idolized. While other girls her age were coached by their fathers and played pitch-and-catch with their older brothers, Dottie was **mentored** by her own sharp eye and willingness to study the game. When she stepped back into the outfield for the H. H. Meyer team, Dottie tried to **emulate** what she'd seen at the ballpark.

The industrial league played a key role in Dottie's training to become a member of the All-American Girls Professional Baseball League. It was the manager for the H. H. Meyer team who organized tryouts in Cincinnati for Wrigley's scout. And when about fifty girls turned out to show off their pitching, fielding, and batting skills, seventeen-year-old Dottie was right there, too. So was Betsy Jochum, another Cincinnati girl, who also played for the Meyer team. After the scout had seen what each player could do, he invited six girls to the tryouts at Wrigley Field in May. Both Dottie and Betsy were among the six.

Crosley Field was the home of the Cincinnati Reds from 1912 to 1970. Originally called Redland Field, it was renamed after its new owner in 1934. *Photo courtesy of Chuck Foertmeyer.*

Dottie was thrilled! But since she was not yet eighteen years old, she had to convince her mother to give her permission to go. Dottie was all Johanna had. How could a mother send her only child—and a daughter no less—to the big city of Chicago alone? Dottie pleaded, and finally her mother signed the paper giving Dottie permission to try out for the All-American League. Later, Johanna would admit that she only signed the paper because she didn't expect Dottie to be selected for one of the four teams. With her mother's blessing, Dottie boarded a train from

Cincinnati to Chicago and arrived just in time to join hundreds of other All-American hopefuls.

When it was all said and done, Betsy Jochum belonged to the South Bend (Indiana) Blue Sox, and Dottie Kamenshek to the Rockford Peaches. Without even returning to Cincinnati, Dottie was whisked away by train from Chicago to Rockford, Illinois. Before long she'd have a new uniform, a new playing position, and even a new nickname.

Did you know? The ship that brought Dottie's father to the United States in 1913, the SS George Washington, *narrowly avoided tragedy a year earlier. As it sailed toward the Port of New York, it spotted an unusually large iceberg near Newfoundland. The SS* George Washington *sailed within a half mile of the iceberg. Crew members radioed warnings to other ships, including the* Titanic, *which was also crossing the Atlantic Ocean for New York. The next morning, however, the crew received word that the* Titanic *had struck an iceberg and sunk less than twelve hours after their warning was sent.*

3RD INNING

THE LEAGUE LAUNCHES

"Come out and have the time of your life! See what a fast, exciting game these professional champions play. . . . Forget your cares and worries—you'll go back to the job feeling better than ever."[1]

—Kenosha Evening News, June 1943

PHILIP K. WRIGLEY'S new female league started the 1943 season as the All-American Girls Softball League. Four teams were established: the Rockford (Illinois) Peaches, the Racine (Wisconsin) Belles, the South Bend (Indiana) Blue Sox, and the Kenosha (Wisconsin) Comets. They played a blend of baseball and fast-pitch softball.

At first, Wrigley proposed the girls play in Major League ballparks, temporarily replacing men's baseball. When it became clear, however, that Major League Baseball would continue despite the number of young men serving in the armed forces in

World War II, Philip K. Wrigley (encouraged by other Major League team owners) changed the plan. He realized it was best to focus on smaller cities without Major League Baseball teams. He was, after all, still the owner of the Chicago Cubs and he didn't want fans in Chicago or anywhere to have to split their free time and their ticket money between his boys and his girls. Better, he believed, to stick with smaller cities where folks had less to do with both their time and their money.

Wrigley hit a home run with his way of thinking. Although fans were initially skeptical, and showed up just to see pretty girls play ball in skirts, they soon learned that these ladies were the real deal. Kammie and her teammates were serious ballplayers, as were all the girls in the league. They threw hard; they ran fast; they hit smart. They could steal bases and slide just like the men in the majors.

But they did it all in skirts, making them appear tougher and more feminine at the same time. This was all part of Mr. Wrigley's plan. He wanted girls who could play like men, but look like ladies. That is why the uniform was unlike any other ever worn—by men or women. It was a one-piece tunic dress with a wide belt. The girls wore shorts beneath their skirts, but those often weren't enough to protect them from the nasty scrapes—called strawberries—they would get when sliding into base.

Some girls protested when they saw the uniform. But they quickly bit their tongues when they realized they had only two choices: wear the dress, or take the next train home. Most decided to wear the dress.

At first, the AAGPBL uniform skirts were too long and too flared. Players complained that the skirt got in the way when running or catching grounders, and they pinned the skirts down to keep them closer to their bodies. Eventually, the skirts became straighter and a little bit shorter. Dottie didn't complain much about the uniform. "We got used to it," she said. *Photo courtesy of Midway Village Museum, Rockford, IL.*

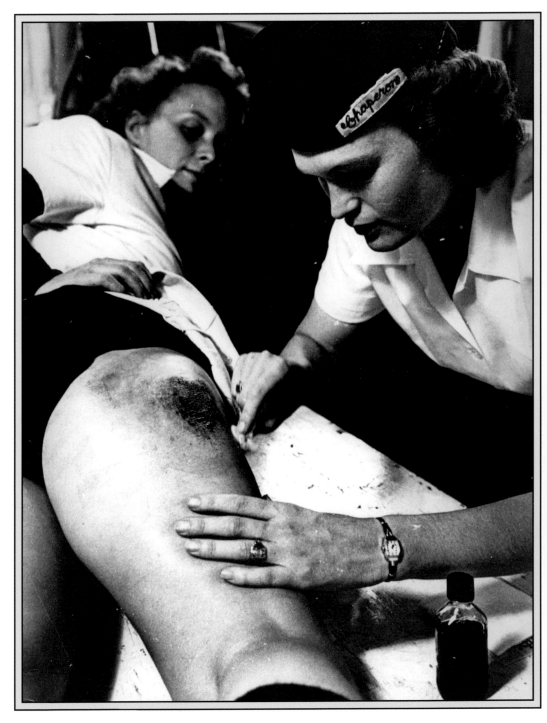

Painful injuries resulting from sliding into base in a skirt were common. Peaches player Lois Florreich receives first aid from the team's chaperone. *Photo courtesy of National Baseball Hall of Fame Library, Cooperstown, NY.*

A Popular Name

WHEN the Rockford Peaches first assembled girls from all over the United States and Canada, the players soon discovered they had a lot in common. Many had played on industrial teams in their hometowns. Most had been playing since they were old enough to hold a bat. And two realized they had the same first name. Dorothy Kamenshek and Dorothy Sawyer quickly decided that only one could be called "Dottie." Dorothy Kamenshek was given the nickname "Kammie" and it stuck.

It's a good thing it did. Before the end of the 1943 season, Dorothy Sawyer was traded to the South Bend Blue Sox, but, by 1944, two more Dorothys had arrived in Rockford. Dorothy "Snookie" Harrell and Dorothy "Dottie" Green were added to the roster. By 1945, the Peaches had four Dorothys on the team when Canadian Dorothy "Fergie" Ferguson joined them.

Believe it or not, the Dorothys kept coming. In 1946, Dorothy Ferguson spent part of the season with the Peoria Redwings, but was soon back with the Peaches to stay. Dorothy Moon was added to the pitching staff and Dorothy Cook also spent part of the 1946 season with the Peaches. At one point that year, there were five women named Dorothy on the Rockford team, and over the years, seven different girls named Dorothy were Peaches.

While no one can be certain, we have to wonder if the popularity of the name could be connected to a series of widely acclaimed books published between 1900 and 1921 by children's author L. Frank Baum. Can you name the most popular book in that series? It became a movie in 1939.

A young Kammie enjoys wearing pants at a team picnic. Skirts in public were the rule while on baseball business of any kind. *Photo courtesy of Midway Village Museum, Rockford, IL.*

Perhaps some girls were persuaded to play, dress and all, by the generous salary offered by Mr. Wrigley's management. The girls were paid between $40.00 and $85.00 per week from the very beginning. By all standards, the pay was more than most women could earn working back home. Also, all their expenses were paid. In Rockford, Kammie and her teammates lived with host families, most of whom were very excited to have a professional ballplayer staying under their roof. When the team was on the road, all hotel and dining costs were paid by the league. In later years, some players were earning $100.00 or more each week. By the end of her professional baseball career, Kammie would be one of the highest-paid players in the league, earning $125.00 every week.

Kammie was elated at the thought of being able to do what she dreamed of doing and get paid for it. She, like many girls, would likely have joined the league for far less money—simply because she loved the game.

Kammie started the 1943 season playing center field, a position she had played for years back at home. After thirteen games, she left Rockford for a brief trip back to Cincinnati. The St. Bernard High School Class of 1943 was graduating, and she had worked too hard not to be among her classmates on graduation day. When Kammie returned to Rockford, her manager, Eddie Stumpf, made a decision that would change her career forever. He switched her to first base.

Kammie quickly discovered that she not only liked playing first base, but she was good at it. As a left-hander, her gloved

At Aluminum Industries, Inc., in Cincinnati, Ohio, women and men work assembling 37mm armor-piercing shells during World War II. In the off-season during her early years with the AAGPBL, Kammie also had a wartime job in a factory. *Photo courtesy of Library of Congress, LC-USE6- D-003716.*

World War II: Women Step Up to the Plate

DURING World War II, women took on many new roles traditionally held by men. With so many men enlisting in the Armed Forces, American ladies took jobs in factories, took over businesses run by their husbands, and engaged in physical labor at home and on the farm.

In baseball, women had stepped up to the plate in a very different way. Sure, the All-American girls supported the war effort by providing entertaining, competitive baseball for their fans. But they also contributed in many other meaningful ways:

- All servicemen were admitted to AAGPBL games free of charge.
- Each game started with the playing of "The Star-Spangled Banner," lining up teams to form a "V" for "Victory."
- Games were held at army training camps and veterans' hospitals.
- The All-American players visited injured soldiers, many of whom were the same age as the players, and lifted their spirits.
- Their first All-Star game was a recruiting event for the Women's Army Corps.
- At other Wrigley Field games in 1944, Red Cross workers and blood donors got free admission.
- They encouraged the purchase of **war bonds** in their programs and other literature.

On the **home front** during World War II, baseball fans were encouraged to support the American effort overseas with the purchase of war bonds. *Photo courtesy of Midway Village Museum, Rockford, IL.*

This sort of support continued throughout the 1943, 1944, and 1945 baseball seasons until, at last, it was no longer necessary.

On August 14, 1945, while the Rockford Peaches were on the road playing the Kenosha Comets, the news came. Not long after the start of the game, play was interrupted with cheers and shouts and the boom of a small cannon. Japan had surrendered. World War II was finally over.

Even amid all the celebration, a small question must have entered the minds of many players and managers, and, likely, some fans. Would the end of the war mean the end of the All-American Girls Professional Baseball League?

Two teams line up for the singing of the national anthem before the start of a game. The two lines converge to create a "V" for "Victory," the hope of all Americans during World War II. *Photo courtesy of Center for History, South Bend, IN.*

hand would always be closer to the inside of the diamond, making it easier to catch balls hit there. Still, Kammie didn't take her new position for granted. She practiced daily, and, in the wintertime, back home in Cincinnati after that first season, she continued to practice.

Once, Kammie's mother heard a constant thumping sound on the ceiling overhead, so she went upstairs to investigate. Kammie was in her bedroom, a ball in one hand, a glove in the other, and one foot on "first base"—her bed pillow, which had been placed on the floor. Kammie was stretching and reaching to catch the ball without allowing her foot to leave the pillow. She continued to practice this way all winter.

Kammie also paid close attention to the St. Louis Cardinals' first baseman Stan Musial and other great Major Leaguers, and then imitated their footwork in front of a mirror. Some say Kammie was a "natural" at first base, but she never let that keep her from working to improve.

By the end of that first season, Wrigley had changed the name of his league to the All-American Girls Professional Ball League (AAGPBL). After all, what the girls were playing wasn't really softball at all, and it wasn't really baseball either. It was closer to baseball because the game followed the rules of Major League Baseball. Major League bats were used, but, at the time, the ball was still larger and the base paths shorter than in men's baseball. Over time, that would change as well.

Kammie was chosen to play first base on the very first All-Star team. It turned out to be a historic event held at Wrigley

It didn't take Kammie very long to settle into her new position at first base. She was a natural! *Photo courtesy of Midway Village Museum, Rockford, IL.*

Field in Chicago. Not only was it the first All-American Girls' All-Star game, but it was also the first night game ever to be played at Wrigley Field—by men or women. On July 1, 1943, temporary lights were set up behind home plate, behind first base, and behind third base. While baseball fans everywhere thought it was fantastic, the All-Star players weren't as thrilled. The bright lights made it hard for the outfielders to see. The lights cast strange

The Rockford Peaches with their manager and chaperone in front of their home scoreboard. Kammie is the fourth player in the middle row. *Photo courtesy of Midway Village Museum, Rockford, IL.*

shadows. Still, the girls were happy to be playing a real game at Wrigley Field!

Kammie returned to Rockford in 1944 to play first base once more. While other girls were traded to keep the teams in the league competitive, Kammie stayed with the Peaches for ten years. No manager wanted to let go of his best player, and, year after year, Kammie continued to prove herself a top-notch first **sacker** and excellent hitter.

Did you know? Americans on the home front during World War II participated in rationing programs. The government issued ration books filled with stamps to each family. When family members purchased specific items, they turned in a stamp of a certain color. If they ran out of stamps for an item, they could no longer purchase it. Some of the items rationed during World War II included bicycles, gasoline, tires, shoes, sugar, meat, and typewriters.

4TH INNING

CHARMED

"The All-American girl is a symbol of health, glamour, physical perfection, vim, vigor, and a glowing personality."[1]

—From *A Guide for All-American Girls*

BASEBALL GLOVE. Check.

Bat. Check.

Uniform. Check.

Ball cap. Check.

Lipstick. *Lipstick?*

When the Rockford Peaches packed their duffle bags for a road trip, they were under strict instructions to carry not only the essentials for playing baseball, but also those for looking their best in public. Philip K. Wrigley was intent on making sure his All-American girls were treated—and acted—like ladies. So important was this aspect of the league that Mr. Wrigley sent his players to school during spring training. Charm school.

O NE item every girl took from charm class was her personal beauty kit, along with specific instructions for its use.

The All-American Girls Baseball League Beauty Kit should always contain the following:

- *Cleansing Cream*
- *Lipstick*
- *Rouge—Medium*
- *Mild Astringent*
- *Face Powder for Brunettes*
- *Hand Lotion*
- *Hair Remover*

Keep your own kit replenished with the things you need. Each girl should be at all times presentable and attractive, whether on the playing field or at leisure. Study your own beauty culture possibilities and, without overdoing your beauty treatment at the risk of attaining gaudiness, practice the little measure[s] that will reflect well on your appearance and personality as a real All-American girl.[2]

In the league's early years, the All-American girls spent their days in grueling practice in the midwestern summer heat and humidity. But, in the evenings, freshly showered and fed, they attended classes held by some of the leading ladies of society. Helena Rubinstein and Ruth Tiffany were called upon to instruct the girls in all aspects of manners and femininity.

Kammie remembered that many players thought of the charm classes as a big joke, an impossibility. They had, after all, had to prove their toughness and their ability to play baseball at a man's level. Now they were expected to sip tea with crossed legs and walk gracefully? But Kammie also admitted that most girls,

Kammie (*fourth from left, first row*) and the Peaches pose in the ballpark in full uniform—including lipstick. *Photo courtesy of Midway Village Museum*

herself included, could use a little help learning social skills. Since her mother didn't wear makeup, neither did Kammie. In charm school, the girls were taught how to select and apply makeup appropriately.

Up until that time, Kammie's travels outside of Cincinnati had been limited. She wasn't sure when or how much to tip for services or what might be expected when eating at a fancy restaurant. The charm school instructors helped the girls learn the rules of society.

Even after charm school, though, Kammie still didn't like to wear makeup. A 1945 Peaches team yearbook biographical sketch of Kammie indicated that she liked her clothing "neat and ordinary" and wasn't much for glamour and fashion. In the end, Kammie and her teammates got a good laugh out of charm school, but each took home what she needed.

In addition to charm school, the All-American girls also had chaperones. Female chaperones accompanied the team when they traveled and served as stand-in mothers to some of the younger players. Many, like Kammie, were still teenagers when they left home to join the All-American League. Sometimes, it took a chaperone's influence to convince reluctant parents to allow their daughter to play professional baseball with the understanding that she would be well supervised at all times.

But supervising the players was only the beginning of a chaperone's numerous responsibilities. In addition to being accessible to players at all times, the chaperones were charged with:

- approving all social engagements
- approving all housing arrangements
- enforcing curfew
- approving all eating establishments
- attending all practices and team meetings
- enforcing the dress code
- and more.

While some players may have felt the chaperones were there to get in the way of having a good time, Kammie acknowledged that chaperones were a necessary and welcome part of the team. "They took care of our injuries, our meal money . . . they were our confidants if we needed someone because we were all very young."[3]

Chaperones were paid about the same as the players. The pay was as good as most jobs for women at the time. Few jobs, however, required the round-the-clock responsibilities of a chaperone. In the later years, when some teams experienced financial difficulties, an older player doubled as both player and chaperone.

By now it should be clear that the expectations of an All-American baseball player were high. Kammie and her teammates, like all AAGPBL players, had a long list of rules they must follow or risk being fined, or worse, dismissed from their teams. Here are some of the Rules of Conduct sent to the players before the start of each season:

- Always appear in feminine attire! No one will be allowed to appear off the bus in slacks, shorts, or **dungarees**.
- All social engagements must be approved by the chaperone. Requests for dates can be allowed by the chaperone.
- Relatives, friends, and visitors are not allowed on the bench at any time.
- Baseballs are not to be given as souvenirs without permission from the management.
- Your appearance at public bars is prohibited.
- Players will not be allowed to drive cars out of town except by express permission of the chaperone.
- Baseball uniform skirts shall not be shorter than six inches above the knee.
- Curfew will be enforced on this basis: 12:30 or two-and-one-half hours after the conclusion of [a] ball game.
- When in uniform, no jewelry, regardless of the type, will be allowed.

League officials may have had rules and chaperones in place to keep players in line, but, as it turned out, the girls themselves were, likely, their own best supervisors. An article in the *Chicago Daily News* about the AAGPBL stated, "Problems are actually few. The girls develop a remarkable team spirit and troublemakers are **ostracized** until they come to terms."[4] In other words, it was most often a player's teammates, not her chaperone, who kept her in line!

Charm school ended after the first three years, but the All-Americans never lost their charming dispositions. Win or lose, it was the girls' smiles and sportsmanship, as well as their athletic performances, that won their fans' hearts.

Did you know? Not being seen in public without a skirt on was one of the toughest rules for the AAGPBL girls to follow. When the bus would stop during a road trip—even if it were in the middle of the night—the girls had to put on a skirt over their shorts or pants (and roll up their pants) before leaving the bus. All this, just to visit the ladies' room! Sometimes they did and occasionally they didn't—depending upon how certain they were their chaperone was asleep.

5TH INNING

LET'S PLAY BALL!

"In 1943 a group of Chicago promoters started something new in sports—the All-American Girls Professional Ball League. The result is something to make a male sandlotter blink."[1]

—*Life* magazine, 1945

I T MAY HAVE been the skirted uniforms or the pretty young ladies that got America's attention at first, but fans continued to pay 75 cents for adults and 25 cents for children to watch the girls play. They supported the All-American Girls Professional Baseball League for several reasons, but most of all because this was top-notch baseball.

And baseball it was. Although the game started out much like softball, many changes occurred over the years.

For starters, the size of ball they used kept shrinking. Starting with a softball-sized ball, the league eventually used the same size ball as Major League Baseball.

Kammie warms up before a game at Beyer Stadium. *Photo courtesy of Midway Village Museum, Rockford, IL.*

Players in the All-American League watched the game slowly evolve from softball to baseball, as evidenced by the size of the ball used from the start of the league until it ended twelve years later. *Reproduced from the original photograph by permission of Department of Rare Books and Special Collections, Hesburgh Libraries, University of Notre Dame.*

Year	Ball Size
1943	12 inches
Mid-1944–45	11 ½ inches
1946–47	11 inches
1948	10 ⅜ inches
1949–53	10 inches
Mid-1954	9 inches

The pitching style changed from a softball-style underhand pitch, to the unusual-looking sidearm pitch, to the baseball-style overhand pitch used by men's baseball.

Year	Pitching Style
1943–46	underhand
1947	sidearm
1948–54	overhand

And the distance between bases got longer and longer, meaning the girls had farther to run after each hit. (And farther to go to steal a base!)

Year	Length of the Base Path
1943	65 feet
Mid-1944–45	68 feet
1946–47	70 feet
1948–52	72 feet
1953	75 feet
Mid-1954	85 feet

Kammie was around to see most of those changes. She played for the Rockford Peaches from 1943 to 1951. She sat out the 1952 season with a back injury, but returned for her final season in 1953.

Over the years, more teams were added to the AAGPBL. Kammie and the Rockford Peaches traveled through Wisconsin, Illinois, Indiana, and Michigan by bus to get to games on the road against teams with names such as the Daisies, Lassies, Chicks, Belles, and Sallies. The league had rules against hanging out with players from other teams during the season. The management wanted to maintain a competitive spirit between the teams, and it wouldn't look good if the girls appeared to be friendly with one another off the field. After the league ended, though, many AAGPBL players—even those from opposing teams—shared lifelong friendships.

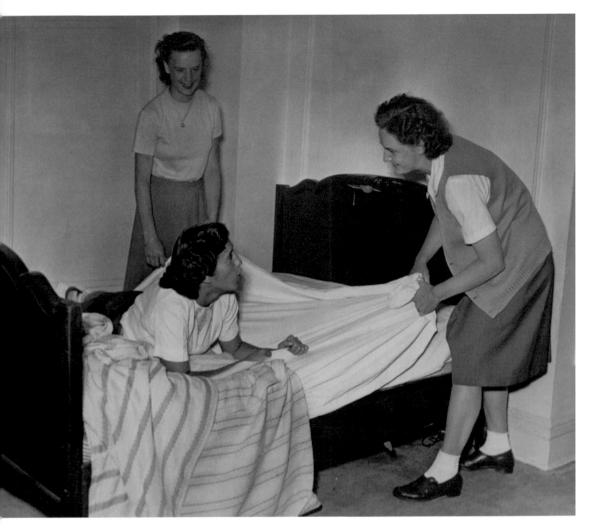

Kammie *(lying across the bed)* and her teammates find a little time for horsing around while on the road. *Photo courtesy of Midway Village Museum, Rockford, IL.*

Playing professional baseball meant being committed to your sport and your team. It was a demanding schedule. Often the girls played games every day of the week and doubleheaders on Sundays. It was typical to play more than one hundred games each season. With little downtime, one might think that the long bus trips between cities would be a welcome break from long, hard practices. But many players found the bus rides to be the most difficult part of their AAGPBL experience. The trips were often long and boring. It was hard to sleep on the bus, and often they would arrive in a new city just in time to head to the locker room and get ready for a game.

One manager named Bill Allington, who managed the Peaches eight of the twelve years they existed, saw road trips as a perfect opportunity for studying. Studying baseball, of course! Every morning after breakfast, he gave the players ten questions and they would have to scour the baseball rulebook for the answers. After writing the answers, the team discussed each rule in team meetings.

"Our team knew the rules of baseball," said one of Kammie's teammates, Helen "Sis" Waddell Wyatt. "When you went to argue with an umpire, you knew what the heck you were talking about!"[2]

Kammie thought Bill Allington was a great manager and an excellent teacher. But she also remembered that under Mr. Allington's management, there was little room for fun. He drove his players hard, sometimes too hard. Sometimes he and Kammie disagreed, but they showed one another respect. In the end, it was Mr. Allington's high expectations of Kammie and her team-mates that helped the Peaches win four postseason champion-ships in 1945, 1948, 1949, and 1950.

When Kammie and the Peaches played in Rockford, they packed their home stands. Beyer Stadium was used for many sports, including high school football, but when the Peaches

A usually serious Kammie finds something to laugh about with Peaches manager Bill Allington. *Photo courtesy of National Baseball Hall of Fame Library, Cooperstown, NY.*

A Rookie's Tale

HELEN "Sis" Waddell Wyatt played two years for the Peaches: 1950 and 1951. As a twenty-year-old rookie from Pennsylvania, she was originally assigned to play for the South Bend (Indiana) Blue Sox, but the day before the season began, she was traded to the Rockford Peaches. Before she knew it, she was at the Peach Orchard, playing her first game with the All-American Girls Professional Baseball League.

"In the first game I ever played for the Rockford Peaches, they put me in at third base. Here I was a rookie, and they hit one down to me, and I threw it over to Kammie. I **one-hopped** it over to first base. So, when we came in to take our turn at bat, Kammie came up to me and she said, 'Now, Sis, just fire it. Throw it as hard as you can. I'll catch anything you can throw.' And I said, 'Okay, Kam.'

"So when we went back out on the field to take our base again, they hit me another one down at third. I picked it up. Now you have to understand there was a fence about ten feet from the field and then there were bleachers behind that. So when I picked that sucker up, I threw it clear over the fence, clear over the bleachers. I think they're still looking for that ball over there in the trees somewhere.

"So we came back in to take our bats again, and Kammie came right up to me. I thought she was going to yell at me, because she was a veteran, and I was just a dumb rookie trying to do this thing! Well, she put her hand on my shoulder and looked at me and said, 'Now, Sis, I told you I could catch most anything, but that was just a little high. If you could get it down just a little bit, I think I can catch it, and we'll go on, okay?'

"And that's the way Kammie was all the time. You couldn't find a better person to play ball with."[4]

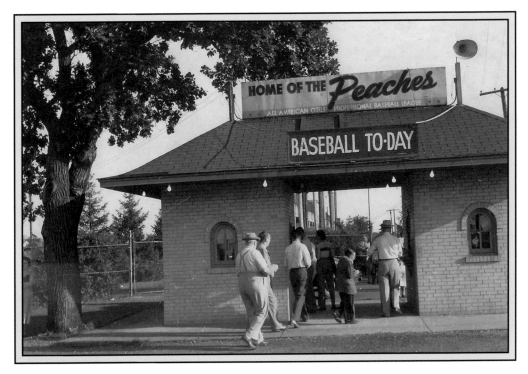

The sign at the ticket booth at the Peach Orchard—Beyer Stadium—announces it is game day in Rockford for the Peaches. *Photo courtesy of Midway Village Museum, Rockford, IL.*

were in town it became the "Peach Orchard" to adoring fans. Only Rockford, Illinois, and South Bend, Indiana, kept their AAGPBL teams throughout the league's entire existence. Much credit is given to the people of Rockford for supporting their team for so many years.

Kammie loved playing for the Rockford Peaches. Over time she became a leader on the team—in part because of her incredible playing ability, but also because of her willingness to help others. Kammie was a thinker. After each game, and especially after a loss, she and the other veterans would start a discussion about what they could have done differently. The rookies always

The Peach Orchard at night. The AAGPBL played a lot of night games during the week and doubleheaders on weekends. *Photo courtesy of Midway Village Museum, Rockford, IL*

listened. Did they choose the right plays? What **errors** did they make? How could they do things differently next time? To Kammie, baseball was as much a mental game as a physical one.

A 1947 baseball program tells why the fans cheered for their team and its many players named Dorothy:

> *"The Four Dorothys walked away with **the lion's share** of applause in the Peoria tassels last week. Dottie Kamenshek electrified the crowd by stealing bases like an antelope and scoring two runs; Dottie Ferguson boosted Kammy along on the route on four occasions during the Redwings series; Dottie Green limped*

Kammie *(far right)* leans in to be in this **dugout** photo with her teammates.
Photo courtesy of Midway Village Museum, Rockford, IL.

> *into the stands Friday night, her leg in a cast, took a long bow*
> *when spectators noticed her gameness, and Snooky (Dorothy)*
> *Harrell performed circus catches and ballet-like throws to retire*
> *the opposition on three occasions.*"[3]

Champions were made when players listened to and learned from older players. And with Kammie's guidance, the Peaches held the League Championship more than any other AAGPBL team.

Did you know? Many of the newspaper articles, baseball programs, and advertisements were inconsistent in their spelling of names and nicknames. They often used "Kammie" or "Kammy" and "Dottie" or "Dotty" interchangeably—sometimes within the same document! Even Kammie's baseball cards, made by two different card companies, disagreed on the spelling of her name. Since Kammie used "ie" when she signed her name, so did we.

6TH INNING

ALL-AMERICANS TRAVEL ALL OVER THE AMERICAS

"Havana was real good. Those people were just bug-eyed. They just couldn't believe women could play ball like that!"[1]

—Doris Sams, nine-year player
for Muskegon and Kalamazoo

I N THE SPRING of 1947 Kammie and the rest of the All-American girls, along with their managers and chaperones, packed their suitcases and climbed aboard trains headed south. They were on their way to their annual spring-training camp, but this year would be different from any other. They weren't bound for Mississippi, as they had been in 1946. Instead, when all 200 players and staff reached Miami, Florida, they boarded planes for Havana. Spring training would take place in Cuba.

For most of the AAGPBL players, including Kammie, it was their first trip out of the United States. They stayed at the beauti-

The Spanish text and date indicate that this program was from the AAGPBL tour to Cuba. *Photo courtesy of Center for History, South Bend, IN.*

ful Sevilla Biltmore Hotel in downtown Havana. Because all eight AAGBPL teams were in Cuba at the same time, they practiced at two different baseball stadiums.

The Cubans loved baseball, but they had never seen women play ball at the level of the All-Americans! Fans turned out by the hundreds just to watch the girls practice during their first week in Cuba. During the second week, the teams played a round-robin tournament against one another. More than 55,000 Cuban baseball enthusiasts showed up to cheer them on! That same spring, the Brooklyn Dodgers also held their spring training camp in Havana, Cuba, but even the Dodgers didn't draw as many fans at the All-American Girls!

It was hot in Cuba. After long days on the ball field, some of the girls got sunburned because they weren't used to the intense heat of the Cuban sun. Imagine trying to pitch or catch with painful, red, sunburned arms! But the evenings were cool, and Kammie and her teammates experienced what the Cuban culture had to offer. Many players tried new foods for the first time. Seafood, fresh pineapple, and even alligator steaks were served.

For their security in a large and foreign city, the girls were told to travel in groups. For the most part, they felt very safe and welcome in Havana. The people were kind to them.

But Cuba's political situation was shaky in the 1940s, and league organizers knew that someone could stage a **coup** at any time. So, on the May 1st holiday called **"May Day,"** when Cubans took to the streets in chaotic celebration, the players were confined to their hotel. They watched the festivities from their windows. Throughout the day, fans gathered outside to talk to the girls. Some of the players, eager for a cold Coca-Cola, lowered money from their hotel room windows using bed sheets and the wastepaper basket. Soon, a fan would reappear with bottles of soda to be lifted up to the players!

Because of the success of the 1947 spring-training trip to Cuba, league officials allowed four teams to participate in five nights of spring-training tournament games in Havana again in 1948. Before that, though, some of the All-Americans returned to Cuba in the fall of 1947 for a postseason **exhibition** tour. Kammie was among the stars who went back to Cuba for nine days of ballplaying in late September and early October.

In January of 1948, when snow was flying in Rockford, Illinois, and many other AAGPBL cities, Kammie and a group of players headed to South America to play nine games against the Latin American Feminine Basebol teams. When Kammie returned from that trip, she barely had time to repack her suitcase

Kammie *(second from left, in hat)* is ready to board a bus with her teammates on one of their Central and South American tours. *Photo courtesy of Midway Village Museum, Rockford, IL.*

before taking off again! In February, she and many of the same players left for Cuba and Puerto Rico.

Kammie's travels didn't stop there. In 1949, a Central and South American tour was scheduled and Kammie was on board. In late January, the players arrived in Guatemala. In the weeks ahead, they would play games in Nicaragua, Costa Rica, Panama, Venezuela, and Puerto Rico. While Kammie loved the opportunity to play baseball in warm climates during the middle of the winter, she wasn't thrilled about the tiny twin-engine planes the

Cuba, Then and Now

IN 1947, Cuba was a popular tourist destination. Located just ninety miles south of the Florida Keys, it was an easy trip for Americans looking for sunshine and tropical breezes.

Cuba and the United States had a diplomatic relationship. In 1898, the United States Army, led by Colonel Theodore Roosevelt and his Rough Riders, helped Cuban soldiers gain independence from Spain. Nearly fifty years later, Cuba was still independent and under democratic leadership. The battlefield at San Juan Hill was a popular site for American tourists to visit while in Cuba.

A 1947 travel film shows Havana, a city filled with culture and booming with opportunities for entertainment and shopping. Cuba's successful production of sugar, pineapple, and tobacco meant Havana's harbor bustled with ships exporting goods, mostly to America. The University of Havana, where some of the AAGPBL players practiced and played, was a leading international university.

These were some of the best times for Cuba. But they didn't last. In the 1950s, there was much political unrest in Cuba and relations with the United States became strained. In the 1960s, Cuban leader Fidel Castro allied Cuba with the Soviet Union and communism. America no longer traded goods with Cuba. Tourism to the island ended. The economy went sour, and many Cubans fled their country. By the mid-1980s, more than a million people had left Cuba.

Today, Cuba is a mystery to most Americans. It is not a country we can freely visit. Many Cuban Americans have extended family back in Cuba they long to see. Perhaps someday, both America and Cuba will rediscover the friendship they enjoyed when 200 young female baseball players descended on Havana for spring training.

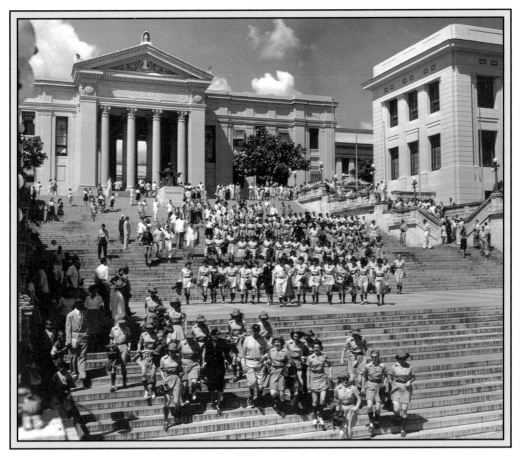

In 1947, more than 200 players from the AAGPBL participated in games at the University of Havana in Cuba. *Photo courtesy of Betsy Jochum.*

girls took from city to city while on tour. Once, the plane in which they were riding had to return to the airport because it was overweight and couldn't fly. No one had bothered to weigh their luggage before loading the plane!

In Central and South America, just like at home, Kammie was a fan favorite. On one tour, artist Evelio Villegas created an enormous oil painting from a photograph of Kammie jumping to catch a ball. The painting was sent ahead from city to city as

An enormous rendition of Kammie in mid-catch hangs at the Midway Village Museum in Rockford, Illinois. *Painting by Evelio Villegas. Photo courtesy of Midway Village Museum, Rockford, IL.*

a promotional piece, and Kammie knew nothing about it until one day she spotted it in a store window. Kammie was a bit taken aback by the painting's size. She went into the store and convinced the store's owner to let her have it. It was shipped back to the United States. Still not sure what to do with something of such daunting proportions, Kammie kept it under her mattress for years. It was stiff and it made a good bed board!

After moving the painting from Cincinnati to Milwaukee to Grand Rapids and eventually to California—all the while using it as a bed board—Kammie finally decided to donate it to the Midway Village Museum in Rockford, Illinois, where it now hangs beside a similar photograph of Kammie jumping to catch a baseball.

After she retired from baseball, Kammie had her baseball glove bronzed. Friends say she used it as a doorstop. It's easy to see a pattern here, isn't it? Kammie never let her fame go to her head. She remained humble throughout her entire life.

Did you know? The reason the Brooklyn Dodgers trained in Cuba in the spring of 1947 was to protect one of their newest players. Jackie Robinson had just become the first African American to join a Major League Baseball club, and the team was not quite sure how Americans would react, especially in the American South where racial tensions were higher. So, the Dodgers took to sunny Cuba for their spring training.

7TH INNING

THE FINEST PLAYER IN THE LEAGUE

"If she was a man, she would have been in the Major Leagues."[1]

—Charlene O'Brien, Peaches batgirl

DOROTHY "KAMMIE" Kamenshek was without a doubt a baseball star. Night after night, the people of Rockford turned out to see the now-famous first sacker make catches and hit like no other player had ever hit in Beyer Stadium before. Kammie was chosen to play first base on the All-Star team seven of her ten playing years.

As a hitter, she was amazing. Kammie was the league's best batter in 1946 with an average of .316. She won the league's batting trophy again the next year with an average of .306. Kammie bought her own bat when she started playing for the Peaches. It was a wooden Ray "Ike" Boone 32-inch, 32-ounce bat, and she used it throughout her career.

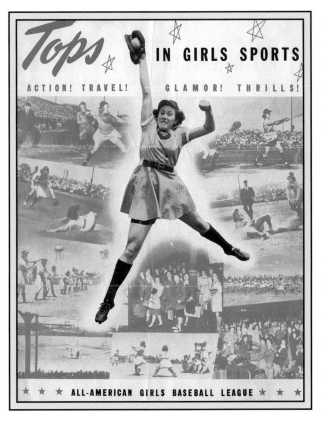

Kammie's picture graced the cover of many programs, magazines, and newspapers during her playing years. *Photo courtesy of Center for History, South Bend, IN.*

At bat, Kammie could do just about anything, but only because she was willing to practice. She was a perfectionist and so was Peaches manager Bill Allington. So, when Kammie wanted to learn to bunt the baseball, Mr. Allington spent hours with her. He taught her how to bunt until she had perfected a drag bunt, which worked quite well for a left-handed hitter. Mr. Allington would lay a handkerchief down toward first or third base and Kammie would practice until she could drop the ball right on the small square of fabric. Years later, teammates and opponents remembered Kammie's ability to bunt the ball like no other player. "Kammie could drag that ball halfway down to first base!"[2] South Bend player Betsy Jochum recalled.

Speed was definitely one of Kammie's best assets. She was so quick on her feet that in the 1946 season, she was able to steal 109

This photo, captioned "Peaches Pin Pennant Hopes on Bats," shows *(left to right)* Ruth Richard, Dottie Kamenshek, Eleanor Callow, and Alice Pollitt, four of the league's top ten batters at the time—and all belonging to the Peaches. *Photo courtesy of the* Rockford Register Star.

bases in 107 games. If you attended a game that year, chances were good you would see Kammie steal at least one base.

This kind of skill was bound to earn Kammie a lot of attention, and attention wasn't exactly what the quiet Cincinnati girl was looking for. In fact, Kammie had a hard time adjusting to being recognized by complete strangers in public. It scared her when people she'd never met before spoke to her, especially in

Kammie stops outside the locker room to sign an autograph for an admiring young fan. *Photo courtesy of Midway Village Museum, Rockford, IL.*

Kammie's Stats Tell the Story

All-Star First Baseman: 1943, 1946, 1947, 1948, 1949, 1950, 1951

AAGPBL Batting Champion: 1946, 1947

Lifetime **At-Bats**: 3,736, with only 81 **strikeouts**

Lifetime **Batting Average**: .293

Lifetime Errors: 192 in 1,005 games

Lifetime **Putouts**: 10,423 in 1,005 games

Lifetime Fielding Average: .982

Most hits in the league: 1946—129 hits

Most **singles** in the league:	1945	102 singles
	1946	120 singles
	1948	113 singles
Fewest strikeouts in the league:	1944	6 strikeouts
	1946	10 strikeouts
	1947	6 strikeouts
	1948	14 strikeouts
Most at-bats in the league:	1944	447
	1945	419

her early years in the league. Sometimes, she didn't answer them because she wasn't sure what she should say. She worried that her shyness would be interpreted as rudeness. Although it was never easy for Kammie to be in the spotlight, she eventually got used to the fact that she was well-known in Rockford and beyond.

Kammie had to get used to it. The spotlight that was on her only got brighter the more she played. The summer of 1950 stood out as one of Kammie's brightest for two reasons.

It was unusually chilly for an August evening, but fans of the Rockford Peaches grabbed their jackets and hats and did what they always did when their girls were in town. They headed down to Beyer Stadium, the Peach Orchard, to cheer on their team. August 19, 1950, was not just any night for the Rockford Peaches. It was a special night, a night that had been talked about and even advertised for weeks. It was "Kamenshek night" at the ballpark.

One newspaper advertisement read,

"Come on, Fans! MAKE IT A RECORD CROWD ON KAMENSHEK NIGHT! Kammie has brought fame to Rockford all over the country because of her outstanding ability as a ball player. Let's all show her how happy we are that she is playing with the Peaches!"[3]

The fans responded. More than 3,000 people showed up to pay tribute to their star. They showered her with praise and gifts. A large ceramic piggy bank was placed at the stadium entrance where fans could place their "quarters, half dollars, or folding money." By the end of the evening, $780.69 was collected for Kammie's college fund. Her teammates gave their own money to give Kammie a $50 war bond. Another war bond was presented to her by her mother.

In addition to money, Kammie received many gifts, including flowers and an electric cooker. There were so many gifts a truck was needed to carry them out of the Peach Orchard!

Kammie beams as her mother, Johanna, is given an orchid by the president of the AAGPBL, Fred Leo, on "Kamenshek night" at Beyer Stadium. *Photo courtesy of the* Rockford Register Star.

Many politicians and some All-American League administrators were in attendance, but Kammie was most excited to see Ohio family members there. Kammie's mother, Johanna, was accompanied by Kammie's aunt and uncle, Mr. and Mrs. Anton Bandenburg, and several cousins. The youngest cousin, Tom, was only eight years old. He sat in the stands in awe of the crowd, the ballplayers, and, especially, his cousin, whom he knew as "Dorothy." To Tom and his brother Dan, Dorothy Kamenshek wasn't a star. She was simply their older cousin.

But that evening, young Tom got a small taste of Dorothy's fame, sharing the spotlight with his cousin for a brief moment. When the announcer introduced Kammie's Ohio family in the crowd, Tom stood proudly and took a bow. It was an evening he would never forget.

Johanna was also proud. If she'd had even a single regret about allowing her only child to leave home at seventeen years old to pursue a career in professional baseball, it would have melted away in the warmth of the applause and smiles of Kammie's adoring fans.

One of the most appreciated gifts of the evening came from a surprising source. The Rockford Peaches' opponent that evening was the Grand Rapids Chicks. The Michigan team had seen some financial challenges in recent months, and because of that, it had been three weeks since the players had been paid. Despite their own financial hardship, the Chicks dug deeply into their own pocketbooks and took up a donation to honor the girl who was, at that time, considered the best player in women's baseball.

AN INCREDIBLE OFFER

That same summer, Kammie attracted national attention when a former star first baseman for the New York Yankees named Wally Pipp made a comment about her that would be repeated over and over again for many years. He called Kammie "the fanciest fielding first baseman I've ever seen, man or woman."[4]

Wally Pipp's words made baseball fans everywhere take note of the Peaches' star player. In Fort Lauderdale, Florida, officials for a men's minor league team were especially interested in Kammie. It didn't take long for them to contact both Kammie and the AAGPBL. They wanted to do something that hadn't been done before. They wanted Kammie to come to Florida and play for them. On a men's team!

The All-American Girls Professional Baseball League was not about to give up their best player. They turned down the offer immediately, which was just fine with Kammie. She had several reasons why she didn't want to play with a men's team.

First, the base paths were still longer in men's baseball than in the women's league. Kammie was worried about running the extra distance on a day-in, day-out basis. Second, male players would be bigger than her current competitors. They would outweigh her by more than sixty pounds and stand more than half a foot taller than her. Though she felt her baseball skills could stand up when playing against men, she knew that, physically, her size wouldn't allow her to be competitive.

Finally, though it was hard to believe, Kammie was actually making more money playing for the All-American Girls Professional Baseball League than she would have made playing in the men's minor league. It didn't make good financial sense to leave her team.

The Rockford Peaches won the Championships in 1945, 1948, 1949, and 1950, more than any other team in the AAGPBL. Shown in this photograph of the 1949 championship team are: *(first row, left to right)* Dorothy Ferguson Key, Melba Alspaugh, manager Bill Allington, Lois Florreich, chaperone Dorothy Green, Charlene Barnett, and Irene Applegren; *(second row)* Ruth Richards, Alice Pollitt, Jean Lovell, Jacqueline Kelley, Louise Erickson, Betty Werfel, and Helen Fox; *(top row)* Dorothy Kamenshek, Dorothy Harrell Doyle, Eleanor Callow, Rose Gacioch, and Doris Neal. *Photo courtesy of Midway Village Museum, Rockford, IL.*

It was a legitimate offer, but, to Kammie at the time, it felt more like a publicity stunt. How unique it would have been to have a girl on a men's team! She was sure to draw a crowd. But she was already drawing large crowds at Beyer Stadium and in other towns when the Peaches went on the road. Turning down the Florida minor league offer was a decision that would be debated by sportswriters for many years to come. What would have happened if she had said "Yes?" Would she have been successful? Some writers are still asking, "Could Dorothy Kamenshek have been the first woman to play Major League Baseball?"

Even Kammie occasionally wondered if her decision was the right one. But, in the end, it was a decision she never regretted.

At the end of the 1951 season, after nine successful years with the Rockford Peaches, Kammie decided to retire from professional baseball. She had been nursing an injured back, even playing while wearing a back brace. Ready to devote more time to college, Kammie had already enrolled at the University of Cincinnati, where she was studying physical education.

June Peppas, first baseman at the time for the Kalamazoo Lassies, was perhaps a little bit relieved to see Kammie go. Kammie had dominated the first base position on the AAGPBL All-Star team for years. Sure enough, June earned the honors in 1953 and 1954. When asked about her predecessor, June had only admiration and respect. "Nobody could play first base like Kamenshek could. She was my idol. My last glove? Dot helped me break it in, and I still have that glove."[5]

Kammie sat out the entire 1952 season, but couldn't stay away. The Peaches missed their star player and so did their fans. In 1953, she returned to Rockford to play again, but only in home games.

By 1953, all the teams in the All-American Girls Professional Baseball League were starting to suffer from two important shortages: replacement players and funds. Major League Baseball had a **"farm team"** system, where younger players were trained to step up and replace retiring players. Between 1951 and 1954, the AAGPBL didn't have such a system in place, and America just didn't have enough girls playing baseball at the level played in the AAGPBL to replace retiring players. With changes in the league's structure, each city that was home to an All-American team had to raise financial support for that team. For some cities, it was too much to ask.

In 1953, Rockford was no exception. Though the city loved their Peaches, it was starting to look doubtful that they could hold onto their team for another year. When Kammie returned to play home games, attendance and gate receipts increased again.

Kammie was devoted to her team, and she didn't want to see the Peaches' long run in the AAGPBL come to an end. When she wasn't on the field, she took it upon herself to be the Peaches' best spokeswoman. She became president of the Peaches Fan Club organization in 1953.

In 1954, the following was printed in the official program at one of the Peaches' home games:

LET'S ALL THANK KAMMY

To Dorothy Kamenshek goes a lot of credit for rekindling the spark of interest in local ball fans late this past winter. It looked like the Peaches club was sure to turn sour after the old board of directors exhausted every effort to raise money. Then came Kammy with an idea and it clicked. Mrs. Joe Newton, Bob Peterson, Pat

AMERICAN
GIRLS BASEBALL
LEAGUE

DOROTHY KAMENSHEK
The girl behind the club

BOOST THE
Rockford
Peaches

OFFICIAL 1954
PROGRAM

All Home Games Played At Beyer Field
- 15th Avenue High School Stadium -

Even after Kammie retired, she was still featured on the cover of this 1954 game day program. Her involvement with the fans and the players helped the Peaches to continue to play that year—the final year for the AAGPBL. *Photo courtesy of Center for History, South Bend, IN.*

Swenson, Harry Carlson, Ernie Peterson and Carl Dahlgren then began to ring doorbells; President B. W. Adams called his 1953 board together; money was raised and old bills were settled. A month passed and prospects were brighter . . . You know the rest—the Peaches are back in the orchard![6]

The program doesn't say exactly what Kammie's "idea" was. Perhaps she suggested the group go door-to-door for support. Whatever it was, it worked. The Rockford Peaches continued to dazzle their fans for one more glorious season.

Did you know? The AAGPBL, just like Major League Baseball, had provisions for waivers and trades. If a team no longer wanted a player, they could put her on the "waiver list." At that point, other teams had forty-eight hours to claim the player. Her own team's management could also change their minds and remove her from the list in that same forty-eight hours. If, after forty-eight hours, no team claimed the player, or her own team did not reclaim her, she was done playing for the AAGPBL.

7TH-INNING STRETCH

LIFE AFTER
BASEBALL

"Baseball gave a lot of us the courage to go on to professional careers at a time when women didn't do things like that." [1]

—Dottie Kamenshek

FROM HUMBLE beginnings, Dorothy Kamenshek had seen a lifetime of accomplishments by the time she retired from professional baseball at the age of twenty-seven. For many, having had such success might have been enough, but Dottie was driven to continue to pursue her dreams.

No longer with her teammates, "Kammie" faded into her past and Dorothy became "Dottie" once again to co-workers and acquaintances. While she was still playing professional baseball, Dottie had started college at the University of Cincinnati, taking

In this 1951 photo, Kammie *(left)*, with Peaches player Virginia Ventura, is seen taking her college coursework seriously. *Courtesy of the* Rockford Register Star.

classes during the off-season. She majored in physical education and health education, sometimes studying between games.

After ending her baseball career, she transferred to Marquette University in Milwaukee, Wisconsin. There she changed her major to physical therapy and did something no other family member before her had done: she earned a college degree.

As a physical therapist, Dottie worked for a while in Hamilton County, Ohio, near her Cincinnati home. In 1961, Dottie and All-American Girls Professional Baseball League player Marge Wenzell went to California to live. Southern California was home to several of Dottie's friends from the AAGPBL, and both she and Marge enjoyed being near some of their former teammates and, in some cases, former rivals.

Dottie worked as a physical therapist for Los Angeles County Crippled Children's Services, where she eventually became Chief of Physical and Occupational Therapy. As chief, Dottie supervised 200 therapists. She demonstrated the same leadership skills in her career that she had on the ball diamond. She remained chief until she retired in 1980. But, just as when she retired from the Rockford Peaches, Dottie couldn't stay away. She returned to work part-time, not as a supervisor, but as a therapist once again, interacting with patients, which she loved.

In life, as in baseball, Dottie Kamenshek was recognized for her superior work ethic and willingness to do her best. In 1980, she was the first woman to be listed in *Who's Who* in Orange County. She was also given the Outstanding Management Award by Los Angeles County that same year.

Always willing to teach others her craft, Dottie was an instructor at the University of Southern California's College of Medicine, Department of Physical Therapy. She was a tireless advocate for the education of children with disabilities, and she helped write local guidelines for the inclusion of children with special needs in all aspects of school and community life.

In November 1999, years after Dottie retired from professional baseball, she was named number 100 on *Sports Illustrated* magazine's list of the "100 Greatest Female Athletes of the 20th Century." She was the only All-American Girls Professional Baseball player to make the list. The entire league could have easily been overlooked had it not been for Dottie.

Even though Dottie had moved to the West Coast, Ohio never forgot its most famous baseball daughter. Dottie was inducted into the Ohio Women's Hall of Fame in October 2001. Governor Bob Taft recognized not only her success as a ballplayer, but also her long career as a dedicated physical therapist.

Dottie's mother, Johanna, also moved from Cincinnati to Southern California to be close to her daughter. Johanna Bandenburg Kamenshek Wiener died there in 1983.

With a fulfilling career and friends and family nearby, Dottie's participation in the All-American Girls Professional Baseball League may have seemed a distant, fond memory. Until the late 1980s, that is. That's when two events occurred that would bring Dottie and her teammates right back into the national spotlight.

Did you know? In baseball, the seventh-inning stretch happens right in the middle of the seventh inning. Historians have uncovered evidence from as far back as the mid- to late 1800s indicating baseball fans stood at the middle of the seventh inning. A more popular tale from forty years later is that President William Howard Taft was tired of sitting during a baseball game. When he

stood, others did as well out of respect for the president. Whatever its origin, the seventh-inning stretch is a good time to get up and buy some Cracker Jack.

8TH INNING

FAME CAME TWICE

"We're more famous now than back when we were famous!"[1]

—Peaches catcher Ruth Richard

THE ALL-AMERICAN Girls Professional Baseball League ended after the 1954 season. After that, there were some loosely organized, local gatherings of players, but, for the most part, the girls didn't see much of one another. Most, like Dottie Kamenshek, had settled into the next chapters of their lives.

In the 1980s, some players began to talk about holding regular reunions. In 1982, the first national reunion of the AAGPBL was held, appropriately, in the city where it all began: Philip K. Wrigley's Chicago. The players had a newsletter, which was mailed regularly to all former players, managers, and chaperones. It was filled with news of marriages, births, illnesses, job promotions, and deaths. It announced changes in street addresses, phone numbers, and, eventually, email addresses.

Once they started meeting more regularly, the women of the AAGPBL decided they needed a Players' Association, and one was formed in 1987. Newsletters had long been **lobbying** for the league to be recognized in the Baseball Hall of Fame located in Cooperstown, New York. At that time, only men were recognized by the Hall of Fame, and the ladies of the AAGPBL agreed they deserved a place there as well. It took a lot of letter-writing, but players, fans, and sports reporters from across the country made their case with the folks in Cooperstown.

Finally, on November 5, 1988, more than one thousand people, including one hundred and fifty former players, stood inside the National Baseball Hall of Fame and waited breathlessly for the unveiling of the "Women in Baseball" exhibit. The mood was jubilant as players and their families celebrated the All-American Girls Professional Baseball League.

The "Victory Song," written by Pepper Paire Davis and Nalda Bird Phillips, and emblazoned in the memories of every player, could be heard over and over again that day in Cooperstown. It was a victory, indeed, to be honored by America's baseball museum—a victory as sweet as any the players had experienced on the ball field.

Victory Song[2]

Batter up! Hear that call!
The time has come for one and all
To play ball.

We are the members of the All-American League.
We come from cities near and far.

The "Women in Baseball" display at the National Baseball Hall of Fame in Cooperstown as it looked upon its unveiling. *Photo courtesy of Midway Village Museum, Rockford, IL.*

We've got Canadians, Irishmen and Swedes,
We're all for one, we're one for all
We're All-Americans!

Each girl stands, her head so proudly high,
Her motto "Do or Die."
She's not the one to use or need an alibi.

Our chaperones are not too soft,
They're not too tough,
Our managers are on the ball.
We've got a president who really knows his stuff,
We're all for one, we're one for all,
We're All-Americans!

A FACE IN THE CROWD

As a youngster in Cincinnati, Ohio, Dottie Kamenshek could never have predicted she would play professional baseball. As a professional baseball player, she could have never predicted she would one day be honored in the Baseball Hall of Fame. And as a Hall of Fame honoree, there was no way Dottie could have dreamed what would happen just a few years later.

Among the spectators at the unveiling of "Women in Baseball" in Cooperstown was a familiar face. Actress-turned-director Penny Marshall was an avid baseball fan. She'd seen a documentary about the All-American Girls Professional Baseball League, and she was intrigued. Curious to know more, she showed up in Cooperstown. After she experienced the excitement and enthusiasm that seemed to follow the AAGPBL players wherever they went, Penny Marshall knew she wanted to make a movie about the league.

Although Hollywood fictionalized the movie's characters, some were composites of more than one AAGPBL player. The movie's main character, Dottie Hinson, was said to be a combination of Kammie Kamenshek and Pepper Paire Davis. Pepper was a catcher, like Dottie Hinson in the movie. But even Pepper said Dottie Hinson was meant to represent the very best player in the league, and that was Dorothy Kamenshek.

Pepper consulted with Penny Marshall on the movie for accuracy. Because of their close proximity to Hollywood, a group of former AAGPBL players who lived in Southern California were invited to Penny Marshall's home before the filming of the movie. Pepper, Kammie, and Marge Wenzell were among the players who mingled with some of the film's actors that evening. It's difficult to imagine who was more starstruck—the players or the actors!

Many former AAGPBL players were able to attend some of the filming that took place in Evansville, Indiana. Those who attended the filming were treated as stars themselves. They ate catered meals with the cast members and spoke to Penny Marshall. Ms. Marshall and the players frequently expressed shared gratitude—the players were grateful to Penny for making the movie, and she was grateful to them for sharing such an inspiring story.

On July 1, 1992, the movie *A League of Their Own* opened in theaters across the nation. Suddenly, a forgotten era was revived. In cities such as South Bend, Rockford, Peoria, Kenosha, and Fort Wayne, old memories were stirred. Elsewhere, many people were hearing about the AAGPBL for the first time. As popular as the league was in the upper Midwest in the 1940s and 1950s, it was an unknown phenomenon to much of the rest of the nation.

There was no more obscurity for the All-American Girls Professional Baseball League or its players. From that day forward, nearly every American would be able to tell something about the movie *A League of Their Own*. The line "There's no crying in

DOTTIE "KAMMIE" KAMENSHEK
First Base-Rockford Peaches

One of two trading cards made featuring Kammie. The cards were not made until the 1990s when interest in the AAGPBL was rekindled. *Photo courtesy of Sharon Roepke, AAGPBL cards, Kalamazoo, MI.*

baseball!" would forever be remembered as one of the most famous movie lines of the 1990s.

If the girls of the AAGPBL thought they were celebrities back when they played ball, they were in for an awakening! After the movie, they became sought-after stars in their hometowns and beyond. Phones began to ring. The ladies were asked to appear at baseball games and trading card shows. Two card companies made the ladies their own sets of trading cards to sign and give away to adoring fans. Some former AAGPBL players did radio and television interviews.

Dottie was once again "Kammie" Kamenshek, and she embarked on what she called her third career. She appeared at card shows all over the U.S. with other former players including Marge Wenzell and Pepper Davis. Kammie was generous and, despite the fact she still didn't relish being in the spotlight, she rarely

A League of Their Own—Movie Fun Facts

AS with most films based on actual events, a Hollywood twist had to be added to the movie. Here are just a few "behind the scenes" facts:

- Not all of the fly balls in the movie were actually hit with a bat. An off-camera crew member used a giant slingshot to send baseballs flying into the outfield.

- In the movie, all of the baseball games are played in the daytime, but in the AAGPBL, most games, except for Sunday afternoons, were played in the evening.

- The movie takes place during the AAGPBL's first year. In the movie, the girls are already pitching overhand and playing with a 9-inch baseball, but we know that, in reality, the first year's games were played with a 12-inch softball pitched underhand.

- The Racine Belles and the Rockford Peaches face off in the first-ever playoffs in the movie. The 1943 playoffs actually featured the Racine Belles against the Kenosha Comets. Luckily, Racine wins in both the fictionalized and real accounts of the '43 playoffs!

- Hollywood created a fictional candy bar company—Harvey Bars—and its owner, Walter Harvey, to take the place of Philip K. Wrigley and his chewing gum empire.

- Most of the actresses did their own stunts and, as a result, got their own real bruises and "strawberries" to show for it.

- The film recently celebrated its twentieth anniversary in July 2012, and even, at that time, was frequently shown on television.

- The movie was chosen by the Library of Congress to be included in the National Film Registry Archives in 2012.

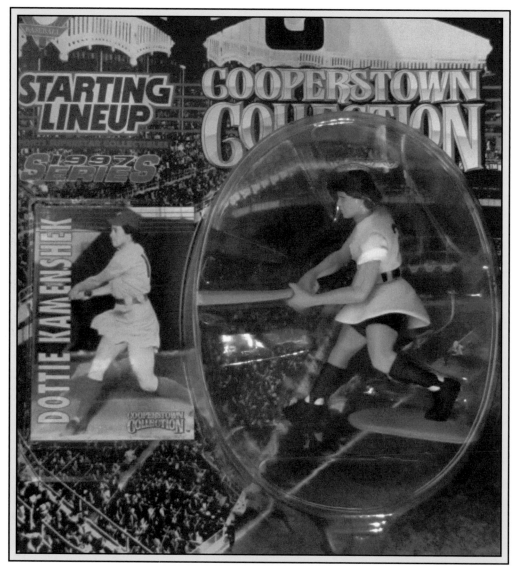

Kammie's action figure, part of the Starting Lineup Series of collectibles conceived by former NFL player Pat McInally, was produced by Kenner Toys in 1997. *Photo by Michelle Houts, used with permission of Pat McInally.*

turned down charity events, especially those at Joe DiMaggio Children's Hospital in Hollywood, Florida.

A leading toy company that made a series of action figures of male athletes created action figures of Kammie and Pepper Paire Davis. Kammie sent one of hers to former teammate Helen "Sis"

Waddell Wyatt with a note that read, "Don't take it apart. It's a collectible as it is."[3] Helen listened to her friend's advice. She still has the signed action figure in its package and in a protective plastic box.

Did you know? When a movie set is in need of a lot of people to fill in a crowd scene, they use "extras." Extras are people, sometimes non-actors, who portray members of an audience or large gathering. In the stadium scenes in the movie A League of Their Own, *many people were needed to fill the stands. They had to wear attire typical of the 1940s, which meant suits and hats for most men and dresses for most women. Sometimes, when enough extras can't be found, cardboard cut-outs are used. In the movie* A League of Their Own, *many cardboard cutouts of two men were placed throughout the stands.*

9TH INNING

WILL THERE EVER BE ANOTHER KAMMIE?

"I think it's a good idea. (Pause.) I wonder if they'll be as good as us."[1]

—Alice "Al" Pollitt Deschaine, seven-year third baseman
and shortstop for the Rockford Peaches,
speaking about the new Rockford Starfires

THERE ARE many reasons why there will never be another All-American Girls Professional Baseball League. The league was a product of its era. It reflected a wartime need for entertainment. It was a new and exciting version of a familiar and beloved pastime.

But just because there will never be another league quite like the AAGPBL, we don't have to believe there will never be another player like Dorothy Kamenshek. There are amazing women playing softball all over the world. And, in some places, there are women playing baseball.

Not surprisingly, one of those places is Rockford, Illinois.

After years of neglect, the Beyer Stadium ticket booth stands sturdy, having survived the demolition of other parts of the ballpark. As a new generation of girls' baseball fans make their way through the gate, the future of the Peach Orchard looks bright. *Photo by Michelle Houts.*

A NEW VARIETY OF PEACH

It was hard to believe that Rockford, a city that once held its Peaches so dear, had gone almost sixty years without women's baseball. Beyer Stadium looked more like a grassy field than a ballpark. Gone were the stands, the dugouts, the bases. The boarded-up ticket booth and a set of concrete steps were all that remained to remind fans of summer nights when bats cracked sharply and fans leaped to their feet with excitement.

One of the Peaches who never left Rockford, Helen "Sis" Waddell Wyatt is now one of the Starfires' greatest supporters. Seen here with Helen are *(left to right)* Starfires players Jessica Johnson, Jossilyn Jones, Elizabeth Layng, and Kristin Tedrick. *Photo by Michelle Houts.*

But recently, the old Peach Orchard has seen signs of life. A new diamond was installed. A **backstop** was erected. New dugouts were added. Why? Because a new team is in town.

The Rockford Starfires women's baseball team is fighting to keep women's baseball alive and well in the upper Midwest. Led by visionaries Greg Schwanke and Steve McIntosh, the team has a full roster, coaches, and an ever-growing legion of faithful fans. The Starfires are onto something big. And right in the thick of

Starfires first baseman Sara Sutherland can't help but think about the Peaches and the path they paved for women's baseball. She's honored to carry on Kammie's tradition of hard work and excellence at first base. *Photo by Michelle Houts.*

Who's on First Now?

WHEN Sara Sutherland was a young girl, her grandmother used to tell her about a group of girls who played baseball when all the young men had gone off to war. They played in a stadium nearby, and Sara's grandmother was a fan. Sara was just four years old when the movie *A League of Their Own* came out—too young to watch—but she did see it when she was older. She couldn't believe it! Someone had made a movie about the girls her grandmother loved to watch.

By the time she was nine, Sara was playing softball. She played in high school and then in college for Benedictine University in Lisle, Illinois. When she returned home as a Spanish teacher, she wondered if she'd ever have the chance to play competitive ball again. She saw her chance when the Starfires organized. Now Sara stands where Kammie once stood. First base. The Peach Orchard. She knows she's got some big shoes to fill. If she listens to the echoes of the past all around her, she'll be just fine.

> *"Baseball taught me that if you work hard enough, you can do what you want to do."*[2]
>
> —Dottie Kamenshek

everything is former Peach Helen "Sis" Waddell Wyatt. A lot has changed since the rookie Waddell fired that baseball right over first base, over Kammie's head, and over the stands. But then again, a lot has remained because of Helen's willingness to share her baseball knowledge and enthusiasm with some new rookies.

On August 31, 2013, the Rockford Starfires welcomed the South Bend Blue Sox to the Peach Orchard for the first organized women's baseball game there since 1954. Fans turned out to see their new hometown team take the first game 5–4. The second game saw extra innings and a well-fought effort on the Starfires' part, but it was the Blue Sox who took home the win, 16–15. Win or lose, everyone present agreed it was a victory for women's baseball.

Did you know? Like most fruits, peaches come in many varieties. One variety of peach is the Starfire peach. Someone was really thinking!

POSTGAME

A VICTORY CELEBRATION

"Kammie had no weakness. She hit left-handed line drives and was a complete ballplayer.[1] She had what I call the three H's—head, heart, and hustle—besides all the talent in the world as a ballplayer."[2]

—Lavonne "Pepper" Paire Davis, ten-year veteran player

FROM CINCINNATI, OHIO, to Rockford, Illinois, from Marquette University to Los Angeles, California, Dottie "Kammie" Kamenshek changed lives. To her fans, she was entertaining, always playing the best ball she could and never disappointing those who paid for a ticket to see great baseball.

To her teammates, she was a leader and a teacher. She'd help rookies develop skills and confidence. She took the "Victory Song" lyrics to heart—"We're all for one, we're one for all!"

To her managers and coaches, she was a dream come true: a star player who remained humble; a power player who never

Dorothy Kamenshek remained an active member of the All-American Girls Professional Baseball League Players' Association from the time it was created until the time of her passing in 2010. *Photo courtesy of William Livingston.*

stopped looking for ways to improve. Kammie was serious and smart, on and off the field.

To her family, Kammie was a source of pride. The first to go to college, the first to achieve such notoriety, and, yet, always the first to remember her humble Cincinnati home and her hard-working immigrant parents.

To her friends, Kammie was irreplaceable. She was loyal and generous. She'd do just about anything for those she loved. And they would do the same for her.

To those who knew her, Kammie is dearly missed. Dorothy Kamenshek died on May 17, 2010, at her home in Palm Desert, California. She was eighty-four years old. Nine years earlier, she had suffered a stroke, but overcame many of the effects of the stroke though persistent determination.

To those who never had the opportunity to know Kammie, her legacy is an inspiration—a reminder that with determination, we can do more than the world expects us to do. She never missed a chance to interact with the young people around her, whether it was to sign an autograph or to provide physical therapy to a child with disabilities.

When a fifth-grade softball player named Emily e-mailed an aging Dorothy Kamenshek with questions for a writing project, Kammie answered with detail. She shared her memories of the All-American tryouts. She described her first game at the Peach Orchard. And, when she felt she had sufficiently answered young Emily's questions, she ended the correspondence with some words of advice.

"A motto I have followed all my life is: Less than my best is failure. Think about it!"[3]

EXTRA
INNINGS

KAMMIE'S TIMELINE

December 21, 1925   Dorothy Kamenshek is born in Norwood, Ohio, a suburb of Cincinnati.

January 13, 1935   Dottie's father, Nikolaus Kamenshek, dies.

September 1, 1937   Dottie's stepfather, Josef Wiener, dies.

1940, 1941, 1942   Dottie plays centerfield for the H. H. Meyer Packing Company team.

April 1943   Dottie attends first-round tryouts for the All-American Girls Softball League in Cincinnati.

May 1943   Dottie is invited to tryouts in Chicago and is chosen as one of the first sixty-four players in the All-American Girls Softball League. She is assigned to the Rockford Peaches.

June 1943   Kammie returns home to Cincinnati for graduation ceremonies at St. Bernard High School.

July 1943   Kammie is chosen to play first base on the All-American Girls Professional Ball League (AAGPBL) All-Star team.

1945   The Peaches win the league championship for the first time.

1946   Kammie is the league's leading batter.

1947	Kammie is the league's leading batter for the second straight year.
	The AAGPBL holds spring training in Cuba.
1948	Kammie visits Cuba, Venezuela, and Costa Rica on off-season exhibition tours.
	The Peaches win the league championship.
1949	Kammie goes along on the Central and South American exhibition tours.
	The Peaches win the league championship.
1950	Kammie is honored at Kamenshek night.
	The Peaches win the league championship.
1951	Kammie retires at the end of the season because of a back injury.
1952	Kammie sits out this season, but remains an active supporter of the Rockford Peaches.
1953	Kammie returns to the Peaches to play home games. She retires for good at the end of this season.
	Kammie becomes president of the Rockford Peaches Fan Club.
1954	This is the last season for the AAGPBL.
1958	Dottie graduates from Marquette University in Milwaukee.
1961	Dottie moves to southern California and begins working as a physical therapist.

1964	Dottie is promoted to supervisor.
1980	Dottie retires from supervising and resumes therapy, working directly with patients.
	Dottie receives the Outstanding Management Award from Los Angeles County.
	Dottie is listed in *Who's Who* in Orange County.
July 8, 1982	The AAGPBL holds its first national players' reunion in Chicago.
July 20, 1982	Dottie and former player Lavonne "Pepper" Paire Davis appear on *Good Morning America* to talk about the reunion.
September 13, 1983	Dottie's mother, Johanna, dies in California.
November 5, 1988	The "Women in Baseball Exhibit" is unveiled at the National Baseball Hall of Fame in Cooperstown, N.Y.
July 1, 1992	The hit movie *A League of Their Own* is released in theaters.
November 29, 1999	Dottie is listed as #100 on *Sports Illustrated*'s list of the "100 Greatest Female Athletes of the 20th Century."
October 24, 2001	Dottie is inducted into the Ohio Women's Hall of Fame.
May 17, 2010	Dorothy Kamenshek dies in California.

GLOSSARY

at-bats: the number of times a player is up to bat

backstop: a fence behind home plate designed to deflect foul balls

batting average: a score given to a player by dividing the number of official times at bat into the number of base hits

coup: an organized attempt to overthrow a government

dugout: one of two areas, usually located behind the third base line and the first base line, where a team sits while not on the field

dungarees: blue jeans or overalls

(economic) depression: when a nation's economy fails, the demand for goods and services drops, and unemployment rises

emulate: to attempt to be like someone; mimic or imitate another

error: in baseball, a mistake that results in a runner advancing a base

exhibition: in baseball, extra games played outside of the regular season for the purpose of promoting the team or league to a new audience

farm teams: minor league baseball teams designed to recruit and train ballplayers to fill needs when they arise in the Major Leagues

home front: the home country of soldiers fighting elsewhere

(the) lion's share: the greatest portion

lobbying: making a plea or appeal to someone in order to gain something desired

manifest: the record or log of a ship's passengers

May Day: the first day of May, celebrated first in middle England as a day of dancing and festivities

mentor: to teach someone; to allow someone to follow in one's footsteps for the purpose of learning a skill or trade

mortgage: a pledge of property as a promise to repay money borrowed, usually to purchase the pledged property

one-hop: a throw that bounces once

ostracized: banished, or excluded from a group

putouts: an action by one player that results in another player being out

rationing: controlling amounts of goods or services a consumer can use

sacker: another word for "baseman"; the "first sacker" is the player on first base

sandlot: a vacant lot, usually in the city, where spontaneous baseball games are often played among neighborhood children

scouts: individuals hired by team management to go out and watch ball games, focusing on players who may potentially play for their team

single: when the batter advances to first base

stock market: where shares of publicly owned companies are bought and sold

strikeout: an out called when a batter accumulates three strikes. A strikeout statistic is recorded for both the pitcher and the batter involved.

war bonds: during World War II, notes sold to the public for 75 percent of their redeemable value. The majority sold for $18.75 and, after ten years, could be sold back to the government for $25.00. War bonds helped the United States government pay for a very costly World War II.

NOTES

1ST INNING

1. Susan E. Johnson, *When Women Played Hardball* (Berkeley: Seal Press, 1994), 167.
2. Dorothy Kamenshek, e-mail message to Emily, December 11, 1999. Dottie Kamenshek file, National Baseball Hall of Fame Library, Cooperstown, NY.
3. Johnson, *When Women Played Hardball,* 167.
4. Sue Macy, *A Whole New Ball Game: The Story of the All-American Girls Professional Baseball League* (New York: Henry Holt, 1993), 8.
5. Merrie A. Fidler, *The Origins and History of the All-American Girls Professional Baseball League* (Jefferson, NC: McFarland, 2006), 29.

2ND INNING

1. Johnson, *When Women Played Hardball,* 166.
2. Ibid., 167.

3RD INNING

1. *Kenosha (WI) Evening News,* June 1, 1943, 9.

4TH INNING

1. *A Guide for All-American Girls: How to Look Better, Feel Better, Be More Popular.* AAGPBL collection, Center for History, South Bend, IN.

2. Ibid.

3. Fidler, *The Origins and History,* 166.

4. Adie Suehsdorf, "Sluggers in Skirts," *Chicago Daily News,* July 30, 1949.

5TH INNING

1. "Girls' Baseball," *Life,* June 4, 1945, 63–66.

2. Interview with Helen "Sis" Waddell Wyatt, Rockford, IL, June 19, 2013.

3. Rockford Peaches baseball program, 1947. AAGPBL collection, Center for History, South Bend, IN.

4. Interview with Helen "Sis" Waddell Wyatt, Rockford, IL, June 19, 2013.

6TH INNING

1. Jim Sargent, *We Were the All-American Girls: Interviews with Players of the AAGPBL, 1943–1954* (Jefferson, NC: McFarland, 2013), 219.

7TH INNING

1. Interview with Charlene O'Brien, Rockford IL, June 19, 2013.

2. Interview with Betsy Jochum, South Bend, IN, June 26, 2013.

3. Newspaper clipping from a player's scrapbook, undated, unknown newspaper. The Peaches collection, Midway Village Museum archives, Rockford, IL.

4. *Peoria (IL) Star,* August 4, 1950, B-2.

5. Sargent, *We Were the All-American Girls,* 207.

6. Rockford Peaches Baseball Program, 1954. AAGPBL collection, Center for History, South Bend, IN.

7TH-INNING STRETCH

1. Barbara Gregorich, *Women At Play: The Story of Women in Baseball* (San Diego: Harcourt Brace, 1993), 95.

8TH INNING

1. Telephone interview with Ruth Richard, July 23, 2013.

2. Official song of the All-American Girls Professional Baseball League co-written by Lavonne "Pepper" Paire Davis and Nalda "Bird" Phillips. Copyright © 1988 Lavonne "Pepper" Paire Davis.

3. Interview with Helen "Sis" Waddell Wyatt, Rockford, IL, June 19, 2013.

9TH INNING

1. Telephone interview with Alice "Al" Pollitt Deschaine, July 24, 2013.

2. Johnson, *When Women Played Hardball*, 227.

POSTGAME

1. Matt Schudel, "Trailblazer inspired Hollywood blockbuster," *Washington Post*, May 22, 2010.

2. Dennis McLellan, "Dorothy Kamenshek/Player portrayed in 'A League of Their Own,'" obituary, *Los Angeles Times*, May 22, 2010.

3. Dorothy Kamenshek, e-mail message to Emily, December 11, 1999. Dottie Kamenshek file, National Baseball Hall of Fame Library, Cooperstown, NY.

BIBLIOGRAPHY

BOOKS

Fidler, Merrie A. *The Origins and History of the All-American Girls Professional Baseball League.* Jefferson, NC: McFarland, 2006.

Gregorich, Barbara. *Women at Play: The Story of Women in Baseball.* San Diego: Harcourt Brace, 1993.

Johnson, Susan E. *When Women Played Hardball.* Berkeley: Seal Press, 1994.

Macy, Sue. *A Whole New Ball Game: The Story of the All-American Girls Professional Baseball League.* New York: Henry Holt, 1993.

Royster, Jacqueline Jones. *Profiles of Ohio Women, 1803–2003.* Athens: Ohio University Press, 2003.

Sargent, Jim. *We Were the All-American Girls: Interviews with Players of the AAGPBL, 1943–1954.* Jefferson, NC: McFarland, 2013.

Drechsel, Edwin. *Norddeutscher Lloyd, Bremen, 1857–1970: History, Fleet, Ship Mails,* Vol. 1. Vancouver: Cordillera, 1994.

ARTICLES

Day, Dick. "Kamenshek Takes Firmer Grip on League Batting Crown." *Rockford Register-Republic,* August 30, 1946.

"'Dottie' Kamenshek Receives Gifts, Tributes from Public." *Rockford Morning Star,* August 20, 1950.

"Dotty Is a Slugger." *American Magazine,* August 1950, 57.

Fay, Bill. "Belles of the Ball Game." *Collier's,* August 13, 1949, 44.

Fincher, Jack. "The 'Belles of the Ball Game' Were a Hit with Their Fans." *Smithsonian,* July 1989, 88–97.

"Girls' Baseball." *Life,* June 4, 1945, 63–66.

Gordon, James. "Beauty at the Bat." The *American Magazine,* June 1945, 24–25.

Marazzi, Rich. "Could Kammie Kamenshek Have Been the First Woman to Play in the Major Leagues?" *Sports Collectors Digest,* July 21, 1995, 130–32.

McLellan, Dennis. "Dorothy Kamenshek Dies at 84; Women's Baseball League Star." *Los Angeles Times,* May 22, 2010.

Milne, Harry D. "Kamenshek Night: Fans to Honor First Baseman." *Rockford Morning Star,* August 1950.

"Peaches Honor Dot Kamenshek at Beyer Field." *Rockford Register Republic,* August 1950.

Schudel, Matt. "Trailblazer Inspired Hollywood Blockbuster." *Washington Post,* May 22, 2010.

Suehsdorf, Adie. "Sluggers in Skirts." *Chicago Daily News,* July 30, 1949.

INTERVIEWS

Bandenburg, Dan. Cincinnati, OH, August 18, 2013.

Bandenburg, Tom. Cincinnati, OH, August 18, 2013.

Burkovich, Shirley. Telephone interview, August 1, 2013.

Center, Rick. Telephone interview, August 18, 2013.

Davis, Ruth. Telephone interview, August 31, 2013.

Deschaine, Alice Pollitt. Telephone interview, July 24, 2013.

Horstman, Katie. New Bremen, OH, July 19, 2013.

Jochum, Betsy. South Bend, IN, June 26, 2013.

Johnson, Jessica. Rockford, IL, July 28, 2013.

Key, Doug. Rockford, IL, June 19, 2013.

Key-Ericksen, Dona. Rockford, IL, June 19, 2013.

O'Brien, Charlene. Rockford, IL, June 19, 2013.

Richard, Ruth. Telephone interview, July 23, 2013.

Schwanke, Greg. Rockford, IL, June 19 and July 28, 2013.

Sutherland, Sara. Rockford, IL, July 28, 2013.

Wyatt, Helen Waddell. Rockford, IL, June 19 and July 28, 2013.

ADDITIONAL RESOURCES

In addition to the resources above, the author also consulted the archives of: the Center for History, South Bend, Indiana; Midway Village Museum, Rockford, Illinois; The National Baseball Hall of Fame Library, Cooperstown, New York; and the Notre Dame University Library, Department of Special Collections, South Bend, Indiana.

These archives contained many personal artifacts, including players' scrapbooks; player surveys; AAGPBL newsletters; and souvenirs, such as programs and scorecards, as well as notes, letters, and cards. Many scrapbooks contained clippings from two newspapers: the *Rockford Morning Star* and the *Rockford Register Republic*.

Much of Dorothy's family information was found via the Ellis Island Foundation, the Midwest Genealogy Center, and familysearch.org.

Numerous librarians and archivists in Cincinnati, South Bend, Rockford, and Cooperstown lent their support.

BIOGRAPHIES FOR YOUNG READERS

Kammie on First: Baseball's Dottie Kamenshek by Michelle Houts

Michelle Houts lives and writes on a family farm in Ohio with her three children and the farmer of her dreams, as well as some cattle, hogs, a whole lot of barn cats, a few goats, and a dog named Hercules. She enjoys reading, cooking, and hiking any place that has hills because it is very flat where she lives. An eternal student, she has degrees in special education and speech-language pathology. She is currently in the process of restoring a one-room schoolhouse, where she hopes to write and someday have a cat she'll name Miss Beadle.

Kammie on First: Baseball's Dottie Kamenshek is her fourth book for middle-grade readers and her first nonfiction book.